How to Become a School Leader
The secret of success at leadership interviews

Second Edition 2018

M J BROMLEY

M J Bromley

AUTUS BOOKS
England, UK

First published in 2013
This edition 2018

Copyright © Bromley Education 2018

The right of M J Bromley to be identified as the
author of this work has been asserted by him in
accordance with the Copyrights, Designs and Patents
Act 1988

ISBN-13: 978-1491042687
ISBN-10: 1491042680

M J Bromley

For Paul, for believing

Contents

M J Bromley

Preface

What is this book about?

True to its title, this book is about becoming a school leader. Although I will, by necessity, explore what it's like to be a school leader, I will not do so in any depth. If you want to know what it's like being a school leader, then I'd modestly suggest you read my book *How to Lead: The second edition of Leadership for Learning* which acts as a useful companion piece to this text. Other books are available. They're just not as good.

This book is about preparing for and succeeding at interview. In this book, I will navigate you through the labyrinthine - and frankly cruel - process of school leader recruitment.

School leader interviews are not just testing, they are akin to Chinese water torture! But don't worry: I'm here to hold your hand, sooth your brow and balm your hurt mind. Together, we'll make sure you're on top form when - and not if - you get called for interview.

Here's a caveat before we start: recruitment is an art not a science and, as such, there is no 'right' or 'wrong' way of doing it. Each school and each panel member will have a preferred style and will be looking for something different. Accordingly, no book can teach you how to pass an interview every time - any book which claims to do so is punching significantly above its... hang on, what's it say on the jacket again? Oh. Ignore that last statement: any book which claims to possess 'the secret of success at school leader interviews' is definitely worth its recommended retail price and should be purchased without further delay. Go on, if you want to be a school leader you have to be decisive! You've already downloaded the sample or picked this book off the shelf; don't dilly-dally, make the right decision and buy this book.

Why should you listen to me?

The advice contained in these pages is based on my experience of recruitment in both the public and private sectors - most notably in education - which spans more years than I'd care to admit (perhaps I'll open up towards the end of the book when we know each other a little better).

I have sat on both sides of the interview table many times over the last [figure redacted] years and have also advised schools on the subject of recruitment on countless occasions. I have personally interviewed - and advised interview panels seeking to recruit - teachers and support staff; auxiliary staff such as caretakers, bursars, and administrators; subject coordinators, subject leaders, and heads of faculty; associate senior leaders, assistant headteachers, deputy headteachers, and headteachers. And

I have been interviewed for many of these posts myself.

Before I became a teacher, I worked in the telecommunications industry where I gained a professional qualification in recruitment and was - amongst other things - responsible for management selection interviews.

In addition to my professional experience, I have also been asked by friends and colleagues - and, indeed, loose acquaintances, friends of friends, and people I've sat next to on the train - to proof-read their applications and cover letters and help prepare them for interview. Accordingly, I've been exposed to more selection processes than is perhaps healthy and have gained a deep understanding of what works and what doesn't.

But, before my head explodes with pride and you toss this book aside in protest at my boundless arrogance, I should point out - in the interests of balance - that I am far from perfect and I've had my fair share of failure, too! I've applied for jobs but have not been selected for interview. I've been selected for interview but have not been offered the job. I've been offered the job but have withdrawn my application having realised it was a mistake. I've got myself tongue-tied and have forgotten my own name. I've been too modest and not modest enough. I've been too prepared (my head spinning with facts and figures, shoe-horned into every answer), and I've not been prepared enough (my head a vacuum).

So I've learned from my failures as much as I've learned from my successes. This book is my way of sharing those lessons and, more importantly, my attempt at avoiding any further conversations with friends about interviews. In future, when a friend or colleague asks for my help getting a job, I'll simply point them in the direction of the nearest bookshop and tell them to pay for my advice like everybody else. Sorry, I digress...

As I say above, although I've had a lot of experience in recruitment, every school and every interview panel is different and so I cannot guarantee that what follows will adequately prepare you for every scenario. Some selection processes, as I say, are tortuous and aim to put you through the mill for several days; others are more relaxed and informal, a genuine attempt to put you at your ease and have a conversation. You should expect the unexpected and be ready to roll with the punches. My strongest advice, therefore - which I will reiterate throughout the book -, is this: be yourself.

Introduction

Broadly speaking, a school leader appointment is made for two reasons: one, because the successful candidate has the experience and skills the school needs; two, because the successful candidate complements the existing middle or senior leadership team - in other words, the candidate will fit in well (without rocking the boat) and will provide a dimension (knowledge, experience or skills) that's presently lacking. So in order to get appointed you need to be right for the school and the school needs to be right for you. It's useful to think in these terms because the interview is a two-way process: the school is interviewing you but you are also interviewing the school.

I can't change the person you are (nor would I want to, you're brilliant) or the school to which you're applying to work. But I can outline the recruitment process as clearly as possible, giving you some idea of what to expect. I can also share some useful tips on how to prepare, what to say, and how to conduct yourself (for example, at no point should you look at your watch and ask how much longer this is going to take because you're having a bit of a session with the boys later).

In short, I'll help you to avoid the pitfalls, to steer clear of embarrassment! So let's get started...

You want to be a school leader, eh? You must either be mad or narcissistic. Or both. At least that's what I was told when, many years ago, I first voiced my desire to become a school leader. The staffroom fell silent, aghast I dared become one of 'them', banished to an ivory tower, whispered about in huddled corners.

There's little doubting that the role of a school leader is tough: but if you want to make enemies and fast, short of breaking the law, to my mind there's no better way than to become a middle or senior leader.

So being a school leader's tough, yes; but the job of a school leader is also rewarding, challenging, fascinating, stimulating, engaging, inspiring, invigorating and countless other words ending in -ing. One thing it certainly is not is boring. If you're looking for the easy life, put this book back into the bargain bin in which you found it and step away from the TES.

I'm guessing you've decided to apply for a leadership role because you think you can do your boss's job better than he or she can. Or perhaps you're bored rigid by your current role, sleepwalking through your duties - albeit continuing to perform them exceptionally well - in a lacklustre daze. Both of those reasons certainly led me to apply for my first subject leader and faculty leader roles. And my first Assistant Headship, Deputy Headship and Headship. Now, whenever I think I can do my boss's job better than he or she can, I know it's time to admit defeat. Or become the Secretary of State for Education. Which is probably the same thing.

In other words, you're ready. You need a new challenge; you need an injection of synapse-sparking (though entirely legal) stimulants. Don't doubt yourself: you can do this. And what have you got to lose? Except your dignity. And your colleagues' respect. Not to mention your spouse's affections. But apart from that, you have nothing to fear but fear itself by requesting that application pack and typing your name in the box which calls for the applicant's name.

There you are, we're still on the Introduction and you already have my first words of advice... type your application. In this digital age, no one wants you to wield that unwieldy anachronistic symbol of ludditism, the 'pen'. From this point forwards, everything you do is being judged and you need to demonstrate you're competent - nay, expert - at using ICT. Besides, the panel may appoint a handwriting expert to interpret your squiggly scrawls as evidence you're neither mad nor a narcissist and therefore have no place on a school leadership team.

Let's look at the application in more detail...

M J Bromley

Chapter One:

The Application

Finding the perfect match

The first thing to consider is the job for which you are applying. Try not to throw your hat into the ring for any old job - not even to gain interview experience. If you want practice, ask your headteacher or chair of governors to give you a dry-run. Only apply for jobs you really want. And only apply to schools you really want to work in. Unless your name happens to be Daniel Day-Lewis don't attempt to act the part of an applicant passionate about working in a school which isn't compatible with you, nor attempt to convince a panel that you relish the prospect of performing the duties of a school leader's role which in reality bores or scares you to death.

A confession: I once applied for a Deputy Headship because it paid more money than the one I had and was closer to home. I got called for interview and, after much soul-searching (and appeasement of my wife who'd have to wait a little longer for those Christian Louboutin shoes she so coveted), I withdrew because I didn't want to be the person in charge of health and safety. I've nothing against health and safety, per se. Indeed, I already performed those duties but I was also responsible for the school curriculum and timetable, for self-evaluation and school improvement, and admin and finance, and much more besides in a small school where every leader performed the jobs of eight people. I didn't relish the prospect of being the go-to guy whenever the toilets leaked or whenever the plug on the staffroom kettle needed testing. So learn from my mistakes: only apply for the jobs you really want and your genuineness will shine through at interview - you'll be able to convey passion and enthusiasm because you'll actually feel passionate and enthusiastic!

You'll need to articulate why the job you are applying for is the right job for you. You need to make it personal and specific both to the school and the role. In other words, you need to articulate how your career to date has prepared you for the job you're applying for. Look at the job description and person specification in detail and try to relate each of the essential (and as many desirable) requirements the school is asking for to something you have already done.

The selection process is no place for modesty and you need to be clear about why you think the panel should appoint you. You should outline the benefits of appointing you and paint a picture of how much better their school will be with you in it.

In order to do this well, you'll need to do your research! Find out what the school is looking for (read the job description and person specification in detail, and - if possible - have a look at the staffing structure to better understand how you will fit into that structure). Find out as much as you can about the school's social, economic, cultural and historical context.

You might wish to find out: what is staff turnover like?; how long has the current headteacher been in post?; what is the school's vision and mission?; what is the school's curriculum like?; how much change has been implemented in the last three years?; what has been the effect of these changes, is the school making progress?; what is the school building(s) like? Is it clean, well-kept? Does the school harness new technology?; does the school respect individual teachers' autonomy or is there a rigid set of expectations for lessons and a library of detailed pro-forma which has to be used?

You should also read the school's latest Ofsted report and analyse their latest performance data (which is available from the DfE website) as well as the 3-year trend data. Read the school's prospectus, too, as well as the most recent school newsletters and headteacher's messages (which are likely to be available from the school website which itself is well worth trawling). If they are publicly available, read some of the most recent minutes from governing body meetings (occasionally, these can be enlightening, though most of the time are anything but; if nothing else, they're guaranteed to send you to sleep in a matter of minutes).

Articulating your strengths and weaknesses

Once you've picked your dream job and before you begin writing your application, carry out some soul-searching. Identify - as honestly as you can without crying - your strengths and weaknesses. For every strength, think of a recent (i.e. within the last three years) example which exemplifies it in practice. For every weakness, list what you're already doing to address it. If you're doing absolutely nothing to address your weaknesses bar burying your head ever deeper into the desert of denial, then start. Now! The best school leaders are self-reflective and are always learning, always facing down their daemons.

If you're struggling to list your strengths - don't pretend to be modest, you've not got this far by being a wallflower - then ask someone who you trust to be honest to do it for you. Even if your list of strengths flows from your big head like water from a burst pipe (you arrogant prig, you) it's always useful to get feedback from people with whom you work closely. You might be surprised (pleasantly or otherwise) by what they have to say and you will doubtless learn a lot about the kind of leader you are or will be.

And if, having consulted your colleagues, you're still not satisfied with your list, then steal some of mine...

Actually, I don't possess all of these strengths - at least not all at the same time - but I know what I look for in effective school leaders and it is someone who is:

• A good listener; someone able to care about and respond to people's needs
• Consistent, fair and honest; transparent and above reproach
• Sensitive, someone able to show warmth and to empathise with people's concerns and worries
• Someone able to give quality time to people, be available and approachable
• Someone able to show assertiveness, determination and strength of response, yet able to be kind and calm and courageous

- Someone able to communicate - through a variety of means and in an appropriate manner - with enthusiasm, passion and drive.

In addition, I look for school leaders who I know will not be consumed by what other people think. That's not to say they are insensitive machines with skin thicker than a Tolstoy novel but that they're resilient and guided by their school's shared vision, as well as by their own determination and commitment to make a genuine and positive difference to young people's lives. And no setback will deter them from achieving it! Let me be clear, though, that resilience is not the same as lacking empathy and social skills! Far from it. I also expect my school leaders to have high EQs, that is to say they are emotionally intelligent. In fact, I'd go further and say that I value EQ more than I value IQ. Understanding how people tick is more important in leaders - and indeed all teachers - than being a clever-clogs. The best leaders, in my experience, do not themselves possess all of the answers, they just ask all of the right questions.

If that's not enough for you, then consider these additional strengths... In my experience, a school's stakeholders - staff and governors, parents and students - tend to respond best to a school leader who: is dynamic and forward thinking; is sensitive to the needs of all and recognises hard work; provides the necessary support others need; trusts his/her staff and empowers them to make decisions and act on their own initiative; does not place undue administrative burdens on his/her staff.

The wonderful Sir Tim Brighouse - former Chief Advisor to London Schools - also has wise words on what makes a school leader successful. He says school leaders need three qualities: energy, enthusiasm and hope. To this excellent list I'd add kindness. Here's what I think these four qualities mean in practice...

Energy

School leaders need to possess resilience and determination, plus an indomitable will and passion for success. They need to show an interest in every aspect of their school, visiting all faculty areas, the kitchens and offices, and speaking to all staff as often as possible. I'd recommend standing in the entrance foyer in the morning to greet staff. This allows them to book a meeting later in the day if they need to talk to you. I'd also recommend shadowing a student once a term to see the school from their point of view. They need to stay calm during moments of crisis, and at such times should be willing to acknowledge mistakes that have been made and then learn from them.

School leaders need to be endlessly curious, continually asking questions rather than providing all the answers. Finally, school leaders need excellent time management skills which means using the diary effectively, delegating where appropriate and protecting their precious time. By managing their time well, leaders can use the school session to walk and talk, and downtime to read and respond to emails and letters, and to do paperwork.

Enthusiasm

School leaders need positivity, especially when communicating the school's vision and reminding staff of past success as well as future promise. Such positivity can be exuded in state of the nation addresses such as assemblies, staff briefings, and open evenings in which the school leader gives a Henry V-style speech (in Shakespeare's play, Henry V rouses his army as they go into battle at Agincourt with the words, "We few, we happy few, we band of brothers; / For he today that shed his blood with me / Shall be my brother").

School leaders need to have an intellectual curiosity, too, reading widely and sharing articles with colleagues. They also need to lead by example, as a great classroom practitioner where appropriate, but always as someone who loves to learn and always strives to know more and be more effective. School leaders can also be role models by performing well in assemblies, visiting form classes and lessons to talk to students and by covering lessons for colleagues to allow them to engage in quality professional development.

Hope

School leaders need to display certainty that their vision will be realised, as if they expect it to be achieved rather than just wish it to be so. They should always seek improvement and keep colleagues focused on the process of school improvement by describing the journey from the past to the present (what have colleagues already achieved?) and from the present to the future (what is their next challenge?).

Kindness

School leaders need to routinely recognise and reward success in a way each member of staff favours (some people like public adulation; others melt into a puddle at the mere thought of it). Celebrating others' achievements should be an everyday part of what these leaders do rather than an afterthought or rare event. They also need to give quality time to people, having an open door policy does not mean being available twenty-four hours a day, but it does mean being able to meet with staff as soon as possible and listening and responding to what they have to say.

School leaders need to be protective of their staff, showing empathy, respecting people's privacy, remembering birthdays, and granting personal leave - without question - when staff have important or urgent personal matters to attend to such as family funerals. They should also set as their default position a genuine belief that everybody wishes to do well and will try their best, rather than assuming the worst of people.

Good. You're making real progress! You now have a much better understanding of your strengths and weaknesses and, hopefully, have a deeper appreciation of what leadership really means in practice. But you're still not ready to write your application just yet...

Outlining your vision and mission

Once you've established your strengths and weaknesses - and before you start your application - it's time to think about why you do what you do... that is to say, work in a school or college. What made you want to be a teacher in the first place, besides the attendant sense of superiority, the fantastic holidays and the unfailing ability to repel people at parties? What are you passionate about, what are your values? Don't fear cliches at this stage. If you teach because you want to give something back to society (and, unlike community service, to be a teacher you don't have to wear a hi-vis jacket) or because you want to inspire young people the way your teachers inspired you, then say exactly that. Just try to hone it later; try to put some meat on the bones so to speak.

In an article I wrote in 2012 saying 'thank you' to the hard-working teachers of England (I'm not sure who appointed me to the role of thanker-in-chief, but I gladly obliged), I explained why I became a teacher, why I do what I do. It went like this:

"I'm not one of those people who think teaching is the hardest job in the world. Before I became a teacher, I worked in the private sector as a manager in the telecoms industry, and before that I dabbled in journalism. I have been on the other side and I know the grass isn't necessarily greener.

"But at the dawn of this millennium, I had an epiphany: I woke up one day and realised my working life was meaningless. I was a faceless doll working in a grey room in a grey building with grey people and for what? What was the point of me? I needed to rebrand! I needed purpose. And so it was a brand new millennium and a new brand me! I was going to be a teacher! I was going to inspire young people just as my teachers had inspired me. I had plodded my way through GCSEs – let down by poor teaching – and my apathy had been rewarded with a batch of average qualifications but, inspired by my A Level English teacher (he was fierce, feared and fiery – but by god he could teach!), I upped my game and got straight As and went off to university in love with life and literature.

"It's true to say I came into teaching to do some good, to give something back to society, to make a difference. But I'm not some worthier than thou type: I don't believe in altruism. Even the people who selflessly dedicate their lives to charitable works get some return for their investment: either they believe they will be rewarded in heaven or else the satisfaction they get from doing a good deed and helping others is in itself a reward. It makes them feel happy. And I don't teach because of some selfless desire to serve others: I do it because I want to feel I'm making good use of my life, that I am doing some good – and that gives me an enormous sense of pride and purpose. And it pays the mortgage. And then there's the holidays, of course."

Once you've articulated why you teach, it's time to (wait for it...) think 'blue sky'. Stop wincing, I hate that phrase too but we both know what it means... imagine a perfect world. What would the department or school you lead be like? The answer to this question is an acorn and, as we all know, mighty oaks from little acorns will grow. This acorn will grow into the oak tree of your vision. The term 'vision' is over-used in schools but is important nevertheless because everyone needs to know where they're headed, what kind of teacher they aspire to be, what kind of school they are trying to achieve. Your journey is likely to be fruitless unless you know your destination before you set off. So, what's your vision?

If you're stuck, as a starting point – using the kind of statements associated with 'outstanding' schools - you might like to consider this whole-school vision:

Our school is committed to the pursuit of excellence, values people, delivers achievements for all, provides a high-quality learning environment, and extends the boundaries of learning. Learning is personalised and engaging; it enables all students to achieve his/her full potential and provides every young person with a gateway to future success.

I must stress that this vision (which I wrote for How to Lead: The second edition of Leadership for Learning) is provided as a template. It should be personalised and made more specific (in other words, less bland!) about what you would want your school or department to achieve in the medium-term (perhaps three to five years).

The next step is to think about how you'd achieve that

vision; what practical, tangible steps would you and your colleagues need to take in order to transform that dream into a reality. These steps are your mission statement.

A mission statement is necessarily longer than a vision statement. It should try to cover all the important aspects of a department's or school's working practices. It should, for example, cover: how it uses data; what kind of curriculum it has or aspires to have; what the atmosphere should be like; how it caters for vulnerable learners; how it engages with the local community; and so on.

Again as a starting point (and, again, taken from *How to Lead: The second edition of Leadership for Learning*), you may wish to consider the following mission statement:

Our school is a place where:
• there is a shared vision of what the school is trying to achieve;
• data is understood and acted upon appropriately;
• students make good or better progress within each year and key stage, academically, emotionally and socially;
• there is a rich curriculum taught by skilled, well-motivated teachers; there is a purposeful, organised working atmosphere, students are valued and their contributions are appreciated;
• resources, including quality ICT provision, are well-matched to the curriculum;
• students are challenged and encouraged to do their best;
• vulnerable children are identified early and support mechanisms are put in place;
• parents are fully informed and are welcomed contributors to school life;
• there is a sense of involvement in the local community and visitors and outside agencies provide contributions to

the school;
* all staff are valued and are supported in their own personal and professional development;
* standards reflect the status of the students: there is no coasting, and realistic achievement targets are consistently met;
* the school is held in high esteem by the local community;
* there is appropriate and interesting extra-curricular provision.

So you know your strengths and weaknesses. And you have a vision for the department or school you're applying to work in. And you have a mission which outlines some tangible actions you'd take in order to realise your vision. In other words, you know the kind of leader you are now and the kind of leader you aspire to be; and you know what you want to achieve when you're appointed and how you'd go about achieving it. That's a good start and you deserve a break. When you come back, we'll start writing your application! So have a piece of paper and a pen at the ready... I'll see you back here in ten minutes.

*

That wasn't ten minutes. I do hope 'time management' wasn't on your list of strengths! Have you got a pen and some paper? Good, there's nothing wrong with your organisational skills at least!

Ok, it's time to start drafting the application. No, hang on... first, there's the covering letter...

Writing the covering letter

Your covering letter acts as your supporting statement. It is your shop window, the first thing anyone reads about you. Underestimate the importance of the cover letter at your peril! So long as you keep it to a single sheet, you can say all the things you wish you were permitted to say in the application form and all the things you're likely to forget at interview when you're under stress.

Some job advertisements state that the shortlisting panel will not accept a supporting statement and instead they provide a section of the application form for you to write your additional information. Even if this is the case - and even though it may well be officially ignored - work hard on getting your cover letter right. It will be read and will help the powers-that-be to form their first impression of you.

Remember: what you say and how you say it are of equal importance so...

The first piece of advice is simple: make sure your spelling, punctuation and grammar are above reproach. If you're not confident about this - and have no idea what people mean when they say you should never end a sentence with a preposition - then seek help from someone who does. Of course, working in a school or college you have the advantage of working alongside a team of holier-than-thou avengers of the grocers grocers' grocer's' grocer's apostrophe: the English department. So long as you don't mind listening to their tutting and suffering their disapproving looks, I'm sure they'll be happy to apply their red pens most liberally in your favour...they probably don't have that much marking to do anyway, and spend all day reading poetry and drinking herbal tea.

As well as ensuring that your letter is grammatically correct, you should aim for a clarity of expression: say simply and succinctly what you want to say, do not attempt linguistic gymnastics (he says rather hypocritically)! Stick to short sentences and plain English. Ensure your letter is also logical, flowing seamlessly from one point to another. As a broad stroke, you may wish to use the following structure:

Opening

Explain why you're applying for the job. Why that job? Why that school? Why now?

Outline your current roles and responsibilities and how these relate to the job for which you're applying. If relevant, talk about how your previous roles - your career trajectory - have also helped shape you, refine you, define you.

Evidence

Address the job description and person specification head-on, for each criterion (the bits that are either essential or desirable) provide recent evidence (i.e. within the last three years) and outline the impact your actions had (try to relate this impact to student outcomes where possible).

Explain how you'd add value to the school, what would you bring to the school that - in your judgment- it's presently lacking, and what's your USP?

Conclusion

Express your personal 'philosophy' - what you think is important and what you think schools should be focusing on.

Outline your vision for the department or school (as discussed above) - relate this to the school's motto and/or what you know it is already trying to achieve.

Express your desire to help move the department and/or school forward and state plainly how you think you can help them to move forward. Try - difficult though it is - to strike the right balance between self-confidence and humility!

The six realms of school leadership

The purpose of your supporting statement is to provide evidence that you meet the requirements set out in the job description and person specification. But it should do more than this. It should position you as a well-rounded leader. So what do well-rounded leaders do?

There are many ways in which we could define the role of a school leader but I think it is reasonable and indeed practical to meld the myriad activities in which leaders are required to engage into six broad categories.

These six realms of school leadership are as follows:

1. Setting a vision for the future
2. Being a lead teacher
3. Working with and developing others
4. Leading the organisation
5. Managing the team
6. Developing external links

Each school and each school leader will have a different interpretation of what the six realms mean to him or her in practice but here, for what it is worth, is my summary...

1. Setting a vision for the future

Setting a vision for the future is a key responsibility of any school leader because they need to have a vision for their school and need to articulate this clearly and with enthusiasm to stakeholders. School leaders need to know what sort of organisation they want their school to be and this should guide their decision-making. School leaders should take account of their school's local and national context, not only in terms of their vision but also in their everyday actions. They should think strategically and involve their stakeholders in their decisions. They need to show conviction of purpose: they must be driven by their vision and not be distracted by setbacks or conflicts.

2. Being the lead teacher

Schools are seats of learning and so leading the teaching and learning agenda is a key role for senior leaders. Being the lead teacher is about having high expectations of all your teachers and about demanding the best for every student in your school. This means leading by example by continuing to be an excellent classroom practitioner who is able to engage and enthuse students, and by being up-to-date with the latest pedagogical thinking. This also means evaluating teaching and learning effectively – through a variety of means including lesson observations, learning walks, student voice, work sampling and the scrutiny of assessment records – and working with others to improve the quality of teaching and learning and to challenge underachievement (by working with data and investing in intervention and support).

3. Working with and developing others

School leaders need to foster a collaborative culture and provide learning opportunities for all their staff. They need to value the importance of continuing professional development through performance management and INSET. They should have high expectations of everyone in their school. School leaders should, again, lead by example and take their own professional development seriously. They should be well-informed and up-to-date with the latest educational thinking and research, as well as government policy (both central and local).

4. Leading the organisation

School leaders should share responsibility through effective delegation. They should demonstrate good judgment, be decisive but thoughtful, and should manage school resources effectively. They should manage their school's finances (although the day-to-day management of school finances should be delegated to a finance manager, this is one aspect of school leadership for which a headteacher/principal should retain responsibility; a headteacher/principal should fully understand the school finances and be accountable for fiscal decisions) in order to ensure their school achieves value for money. It is a school leader's duty to use public money wisely. This is achieved by being prudent, by planning ahead (including detailed costs in the school improvement plan) and by prioritising spending according to greatest need and according to the impact that spending will have on learning.

School leaders should also manage the site ensuring it complies with health and safety regulations and safeguarding. School leaders need to ensure that resources match the curriculum. Finally, senior leaders should manage the school's most important – and costly – resource: staff. This means ensuring that supply meets demand (in practice, this might involve restructuring) and that all staff have the tools and skills they need in order to do their jobs well (this means appropriate training but also evaluating whether staff have the requisite capability and, if not, taking appropriate action).

Leading the organisation is often a part of the job that school leaders find most challenging and difficult because they have trained as teachers not managers, but it is also the most important part of the job if a school is to move forwards and achieve sustainable improvements.

5. *Managing the team*

School leaders should take responsibility for their decisions and for the performance of their school. They should ensure clear accountability at all levels through effective line management structures and by drawing clear links between the school improvement plan and what is happening in school. They should analyse performance regularly and robustly, and give clear feedback and performance reports to stakeholders.

School leaders have legal accountability for what happens in their school as well as moral accountability. They should do what they think is right and should take advice from others – including their local authority and trade unions – wherever possible. But above all they should do what is right for their school and take decisions that will stand up to tough scrutiny over the long-term.

6. *Developing external links*

School leaders should develop and encourage effective partnerships with other schools, agencies and the community. Community cohesion is often misunderstood – or at least underestimated – as only referring to a school offering its site to the local community. Enabling community use is certainly important – be that by leasing your fields to the local football team or by running adult education classes in the evenings – but community cohesion is also about respecting diversity and protecting vulnerable students. It is about understanding the local community and taking account of where students come from. It is about working with parents. It is about bringing the world into schools to raise students' awareness of the world. It is about respecting diversity and inclusion of all types, ensuring a personalised learning programme in which every child has the opportunity to fulfil his or her potential irrespective of socio-economic or ethnic background.

Once you're clear about what constitutes your 'realms' of school leadership, it's time to think about how you embody them in practice…

Providing evidence of your achievements

You will need to provide evidence to support any claims you make in your letter and application, as well as anything you say during the interview process, so for every success you intend to share, ensure you have detailed supporting data. This might be hard facts and figures, say from the government's Assessing School Performance (ASP) system. It might also be quotes and judgments from Ofsted and your local authority or academy trust advisors. It might include evidence gleaned from student and parent surveys. Whatever the source of your evidence, it's wise to demarcate your examples using the six standards we discussed above. So ask yourself these questions, thinking of specific examples wherever possible:

Setting a vision for the future

What project have you been involved in or lead which has improved an aspect of your current school? How did you get involved? Why? What did you hope to achieve? Why was this important? How did you identify that this change was needed? How did you communicate this need to others and involve them in the process of change? What actions did you (and they) take? Did the project go to plan? If so, why? What was successful about it? If not, why not? What have you learnt from it that you'll put into practice the next time you lead a similar project? How did you deal with set-backs or barriers?

Being the lead teacher

How have you improved your own and/or others teaching practice? How have you continued to improve the quality of your teaching? How do you lead by example? Give a concrete example of this. How do you demonstrate high expectations of yourself, of other teachers, and of students? How do you monitor and evaluate your own and others' teaching and assessment?

Working with and developing others

What professional development have you been involved in? How did this come about and why? How do you ensure you keep getting better at what you do? Have you helped others to improve their teaching or develop their knowledge, experiences and skills? Have you, for example, been involved in any coaching or mentoring of newer colleagues? How have you - through your everyday actions - fostered a sense of collaboration? Are you a member of any professional associations? Have you attended or been involved in any local or national conferences/events?

Leading the organisation

Give an example of when you're demonstrated good

judgment, been decisive and thoughtful, and managed school resources effectively. Have you had any budgetary responsibilities? If so, how have you ensured good value for money? Have you any experience of developing the school environment? What health and safety responsibilities have you had? Have you had to have any difficult conversations with colleagues? Why? How did you approach it and what happened?

Managing the team

Have you used performance management effectively to drive improvements in your teaching? What evidence have you got that you've met or exceeded targets? Have you had any involvement in the school development plan? Have you worked closely with the senior leadership team and/or governing body? How do you monitor and evaluate your own performance? Have you monitored and evaluated the performance of others? If so, what feedback have you given and what was the result?

Developing external links

What partnerships have you fostered with others such as teachers, support staff, parents, governors, local authority employees, social services, the careers service, local businesses, and so on? What have you done to improve your students' awareness of their local, national, and international community? How have you encouraged students to respect diversity, and how have you protected vulnerable learners? What have you done in response to the Prevent agenda and to promote fundamental British values? How do you ensure that every child is given the opportunity to fulfil his or her potential irrespective of his/her socio-economic or ethnic background?

Later in this book, in the section about the interview, I have shared some other questions which you might be asked against each of the six standards. The above questions are intended to get you thinking about what you've already achieved so that you're able to provide evidence of your successes in the application form. The list above is by no means exhaustive and the questions are entirely my own.

Once you've listed examples of the work you've done against each of the six standards, you need to consider the impact of your actions. You might find it helpful to tabulate this information as follows:

Realm of school leadership: [state which of the six realms your example refers to]

Example: [briefly outline what you did]

Evidence: [provide more detailed information about your actions, why you did what you did, etc.]

Impact: [provide specific data - numbers and/or quotations - to show the result of your actions]

In terms of providing evidence, it might be useful to structure your narrative as follows:
- explain why you felt the need to do what you did
- state the objectives, what you hoped to achieve
- list the key actions you took
- outline, briefly and anecdotally, the result(s) of your actions
- state what you learned from the experience

As I say above, the data you use to demonstrate impact might include: quotes from an Ofsted report; quotes from a local authority, diocesan or academy trust report; quotes from surveys/questionnaires; quotes from meeting minutes; exam statistics; progress statistics; etc.

It's wise to spend a reasonable amount of time on this task because your evidence and data will prove invaluable, not only in writing this application but also during the interview process and - if on this occasion you're unsuccessful - for future applications and interviews, too. Aside from the recruitment process, such rich evidence of your work will be useful to you in helping shape your career.

The covering letter is finished. Now it's time to fill out the application form...

Don't forget that the form should be typed if possible. Try to differentiate between the standard text on the form and your own words, perhaps by writing in bold or by tabbing along the page to form some clean white space.

Much of the form is self-explanatory - I'm sure, for example, that you know your own name and address, and your employment history and educational qualifications, without relying on my help!. So we will skip to the parts of the form which are not...

Evidence of continuing professional development

Here it's worth taking some time to reflect on all the professional development you've been involved in over the course of the last three years. Include any training courses you've attended as well as INSET and other professional development events held in school. Also consider what opportunities you've asked for or been given which have helped to expand your knowledge and experience, especially if it was whole-school rather than subject-specific. For each relevant example, consider the following:

- how did the opportunity arise?
- what did it involve?
- what did you learn from it?
- how has it informed your practice?
- how have you shared your learning with others?
- how did it benefit the school?

It's advisable to demonstrate that you're self-reflective and always eager to improve, to learn. It's also wise to show how you've applied new ideas and experiences (in other words, articulate the impact the training has had on you and your school) and - perhaps most importantly - how it's helped to prepare you for the role for which you're applying.

The personal statement
Sometimes called the 'supporting statement' or 'additional information'.

Here I'd suggest you refer back to what I said about the covering letter, particularly the three-part structure. Also consider the following:

What don't the shortlisting panel want to read?

They don't want an extended travelogue of your career nor an over-inflated eulogy to your every success. Yes, you need to outline your main achievements (and, yes, you're bound to be biassed) but they want as impartial a synopsis as possible. They don't want to be lectured about your philosophy on leadership and management or about what their school should be doing. And, most of all, they don't want an application littered with jargon and soundbites!

What do the shortlisting panel want to read?

Your letter and application form should be written in a simple, straight-forward style - formal but not too stuffy. They want a brief statement of your educational viewpoint, a strong sense that you care about and are committed to children, that you have the experience required (so use the words that appear in the job description and person specification as far as possible), and they want to know what you can offer them that will help them move forwards. They also want a concise summary of what you consider to be your personal qualities and professional skills. Though it has become ubiquitous in applications these days, it's still worthwhile making reference to the fact that you have a sense of humour (nobody wants a dullard on their team!) and that you're resilient and diligent in all that you do .

Overall, you want to strike the right balance between providing enough detail for the panel to be able to reach an informed, rounded decision about you, but you don't want to offer too much detail that will bore them or lead them to question your ability to communicate clearly and concisely! You want to sound intelligent (nobody wants an intellectual lightweight) without sounding too authoritative. You want to sell yourself (and appear to have taken the process seriously) without sounding too arrogant. And you want to present yourself as somehow different to the other candidates without also deviating too much from what the form asks you to do.

Don't forget: the application process is not meant to be easy - it is intended to help the panel distinguish between candidates. So if you find it difficult and time-consuming then you're not alone and should not be discouraged.

Proof-reading

Once your letter and application form are complete, check them and check them again. If possible, ask someone else to proof-read them for you, too. You should be proof-reading your work for spelling, punctuation, and grammar mistakes, as well as for a general sense of how you sound (paying attention to the 'do's' and 'don'ts' above).

Once you're completely satisfied with your application, send it!

And then wait. And wait some more.

Chapter Two:
The Selection Day Activities

After days and weeks waiting by the front door, the envelope finally arrives. You know this is the one you've been waiting for because it's stamped with the school crest. And you only usually receive circulars and bills.

You'd almost given up hope, assumed your application had been thrown onto the pyre, just another wannabe who didn't quite cut the mustard. But at last they've acknowledged your application. All that hard work - that painful self-flagellation, that painstaking research into the school, all those cold lonely nights spent reading Ofsted reports and governors' minutes, and staring at tables of data until the numbers and graphs blurred out of sight - has come to this.

You know this letter can only mean one of two things. Either 'thanks but no thanks' or 'now the real torture begins'. And now the moment has arrived, you're no longer sure which outcome you'd prefer.

You tear the envelope open and pull out the letter, skipping the addresses and salutations ('Dear blah, blah, blah'...) You come to the first sentence which, predictably, thanks you for your application and explains that there were a lot of applicants... hmm, are they trying to sweeten the pill by suggesting it was a tough choice and you were running in a strong field?

Then you arrive at the killer second line: it'll either say "We'd be delighted to invite you to..." or "Unfortunately, on this occasion your application has not been successful..."

If it's the former, then don't lose heart (or blame me). An unsuccessful application does not necessarily mean you've failed! In fact, it rarely means that. More likely, it means that you were a credible candidate and would walk into an interview for a school leader's job at another school and at another time but that this particular school and the particular personalities who sat around the table to shortlist candidates were looking for something specific that you didn't offer or that someone else offered in greater abundance.

Maybe your experience did not precisely match that desired by the selection panel (you have too little or too much or not the right kind). Maybe you are everything they wanted and, on another day with a prevailing wind, you'd have waltzed onto the shortlist but, unluckily for you, this time there's a stronger candidate who more closely matches the job description and person specification or who matches your experience but has been doing it much longer and perhaps in a couple of different settings.

Whatever the reason for not being invited to interview, you should not be downbeat. You have dipped your toe into the icy waters of school leader recruitment and now have a clearer understanding of your strengths and weaknesses, and are now at the top of your game: you're fighting fit and ready to do battle once more. And next time it'll be easier because you've got ready-made evidence of your achievements and the impact they have had.

If it's the latter, then congratulations! Your application was successful. You offer something that the school is looking for and have the potential to become a school leader. Smile, pat yourself on the back, be proud of your achievement. Whatever happens next, you are appoint-able and your application has impressed someone. Of course, that smile will not live long upon your lips because you'll soon realise that now the real hard work must begin.

So just what can you expect to happen next...?

You're likely to be given about a week's notice, perhaps more. Depending on the school and the role for which you've applied, the selection process could be anything from a half day to three full days. If the process runs over more than one day, it's likely there'll be a 'cut' at the end of day one and again at the end of day two whereby candidates will be whittled down to a smaller number based on how they performed the initial tasks. The selection panel will want no more than a handful - perhaps as few as two - people at the final interview.

My strongest advice about what to do between receiving your letter of invitation and attending the selection day is to make sure you retain a healthy work-life balance and get plenty of sleep the night before the interview. Of course, you'll need to do a lot of preparatory work - like cramming for an exam - but the best preparation is to stay calm and collected, and - above all - to be yourself.

You should also accept at this stage that the selection process will not go entirely smoothly from beginning to end and that you will not achieve perfection! You are human, after all. And an interview is a stressful experience for anyone to go through, no matter what some people might say about how they're 'good at interviews'.

Don't expect perfection, just expect to try your best. And the way to try your best is to 'sell' your greatest asset: you! In other words, the best thing you have going for you is the fact that you are the person you are. If the school doesn't want you then the last thing you should want is to end up working there. You'll find it hard to conform, hard to get on with the job, and hard to achieve anything you consider worthwhile. So be yourself... be professional, be polite, be impressive, but, most of all, be you. Try to be warm, show you care about the job and are enthusiastic about teaching. Don't worry about trying to prove you have a wonderful sense of humour...if you try to force your sense of humour on the panel, chances are it'll seem false and will fail to impress.

Have some pre-prepared pleasantries to utter as you arrive and as you are introduced to the school staff and the selection panel. Try to say something complimentary about the school. Be polite and courteous at all times, never forgetting - even in the midst of crisis - to say 'please' and 'thank you'. You'd be surprised how important the impression you give to staff is: many staff are likely to be asked for their opinions of you before the decision is made and everyone warms to a polite, kind and courteous person.

The best advice I could offer which will guide how you conduct yourself throughout the process is this: walk into the school as if you've already been appointed. In other words, if you're being interviewed for the headteacher's job, then conduct yourself as if you are the headteacher. I'm not advocating taking over, far from it. But I am suggesting that staff - and the panel - need to see you in the role for which you're applying. If they're looking for their next headteacher or deputy head, they're not going to appoint the meek and mild wallflower who melts into the corners of rooms and doesn't engage with others. It is a fine line between being confident and having presence, and being arrogant. Try to stay the right side of it...

One of the other things you're going to have to do throughout the selection process is to demonstrate that you're genuinely interested in (I will refrain from saying 'passionate about') education and have endless enthusiasm for the profession. You're also likely to have to prove that you understand the current educational landscape and are aware of the road ahead, too; and that you are alert to any proposed changes and the impact they're likely to have in school. In other words, you need to...

Demonstrate you have up-to-date knowledge

You will need to demonstrate that you keep up-to-date with all the latest news from the world of education so you should read the education news daily and make repeated visits to the Ofsted and DfE websites. If life's too short to trawl the national dailies, let me help you... I tweet the most pertinent education news and comment (as I see it; it is, of course, subjective) from my Twitter account @mj_bromley. Follow me and I'll help keep you up-to-date!

You need to be aware of the latest education policies and reforms such as any planned changes to the National Curriculum and the system of qualifications, and any changes to the law governing, say, child protection and safeguarding. You should also have a working knowledge of recent and planned funding changes.

Unfortunately for you, the current pace of change in education is frenetic!

Having views on each of the latest education policy changes is advisable because you may be asked what you think of the changes. In such a situation it's perhaps best to avoid outright political commentary and instead to show that you have a considered opinion, and can recognise the opportunities and threats inherent in each reform. Moreover, it's important to recognise how you think each reform will affect the school to which you are applying.

As a rule of thumb, school leaders tend to act as a buffer to unwanted, unnecessary change and yet embrace positive change if it's in the best interests of their students. Whatever their opinion, these leaders are certainly abreast of the latest policies and processes and have quickly instigated discussions with their colleagues and/or governing body about how the school will respond.

In proving that you're up-to-date, don't limit your research to official government policies. Also consider the alternatives such as those policies proposed by the shadow education secretary as well as by interested parties such as, in no particular order: The Education Select Committee (this parliamentary committee provides checks and balances on government policy, it is often a dissenting voice so not to be confused with the DfE); Ofsted; Ofqual; The National College for Teaching and Leadership; CEM (The Centre for Evaluating and Monitoring); Education Development Trust (formerly CfBT); NFER; Sec-Ed Magazine (secondary phase) and Headteacher Update (primary phase); IoE (The Institute of Education at King's College, London); SSAT (Specialist Schools and Academies

Trust); The Teacher Development Trust; The Local Schools Network; and the main teaching unions (including, though not exclusively, the NEU, NASUWT, NAHT, ASCL).

One of the most time-consuming roles for the school leader is to keep up-to-date and this involves reading widely. In reality - although having and modelling a work-life balance is very important - this involves catching up on the latest articles and research papers in the evenings at home. I have harnessed technology to help make this process as painless as possible. I use a paperless system (usually on my iPad) whereby I scroll through all the latest articles and papers (having subscribed to various email lists, Twitter feeds and blogs) first thing in the morning and save the most important ones (as far as I see it) to an app such as Feedly, Readability, Pocket or Notability. Most are then sent automatically to my Kindle which I turn to once my children are in bed! Of course, such a regime is made easier if you're a news junkie and genuinely interested in education policy! But by carrying out these tasks away from school, your colleagues only see the tip of the iceberg - you are seeming to work sensible hours and make time for your colleagues and students - whilst the rest of the job remains hidden beneath the waters.

Let's take a look at all the weird and wonderful tasks that await you during the selection day(s)...

The first piece of advice is to remember that the interview begins the moment you arrive in the school car park! At no point should you drop your guard or be tricked into thinking you're having an 'off the record' conversation. Remain utterly professional and above reproach at all times.

It's also worth remembering that there is not a 'right'

candidate either, only the candidate who best fits that particular school at that particular time. Equally, you may quickly realise that the school is not the right fit for you. If so, you should have the confidence to withdraw from the process. Do so magnanimously by thanking all those involved for their time and for the opportunity to visit their wonderful school. Then explain briefly that you've decided to withdraw because the post isn't right for you at that moment in time and you'd rather the panel were able to focus on the other candidates than be distracted by you. Wish them well with their appointment, hand back your lanyard and go home. Via the pub.

If you stay the course but are not successful, don't take it personally - the panel has not judged you as a person nor as a professional. They have simply compared the candidates and decided which is right for their school based on their needs not on your skills. Of course, you may be competing with an outstanding candidate who is even better than you are!

You should be offered feedback - whether you're successful or not. You should always accept this offer and listen to the debrief objectively. You may disagree with some or all of it but it is, nevertheless, their opinion and that makes it valid. Moreover, it may also be the opinion of the next panel you face so you should try to learn from it and do something differently next time.

Of course, sometimes the feedback - even for the unsuccessful candidate - is wholly positive because you were a credible and impressive candidate but there just happened to be someone better than you on the day! If so, then you should be pleased with your performance and aim to do likewise next time. If you are repeatedly unsuccessful, you should discuss all the feedback you've had with someone you trust and ask them their opinion. You should also try to arrange a mock interview with a colleague who can be more direct with you than someone who has never met you prior to the interview day.

During the selection day(s), you should try to smile as much as possible and speak to as many people as you can, remembering to be polite and professional at all times. You should trust no one: anyone could be involved in the decision or may influence the panel. When speaking to staff and students, show a genuine interest in them but also try to find out what the school is really like. It's possible that the headteacher and selection panel generals will present a very different picture of their school than their troops!

Ask lots of questions of the staff or students who give you the tour and try to assimilate their answers into what you already know and use the information in your interviews.

The most difficult part of the day is often the part you least suspect: lunch! Try to remain professional and to show decorum whilst eating the buffet! Yes, your table manners may well be judged so avoid over-eating and do your utmost not to spill anything down your best shirt.

Now let's explore the activities you're likely to be involved in.

There are many hoops through which you're likely to be asked to jump. We'll start with the panel interviews which are interviews-lite because they tend to be shorter than the final interview, involve fewer questions, a smaller panel, and ostensibly adopt a (slightly) more informal tone.

The Panel Interviews

The nature and volume of the panel interviews you'll face is dependent on the job for which you're applying, and on the school and selection panel's own preferences. If you are not told in advance which panels to expect, then it is wise to prepare for the following:
- personnel, people management (including appraisal)
- resource management (including the use of learning technologies)
- financial management
- curriculum development and design
- teaching, learning and assessment
- personal development, behaviour and welfare
- systems for pastoral care
- safeguarding and child protection

We'll start with some general advice about how to conduct yourself in these interviews then turn to some sample interview questions.

Do not be fooled if your inquisitors inform you that the panel interviews are 'informal discussions' or 'a bit more laid back' with time to 'talk more freely' than the final interview will allow. The panel interviews are still interviews and you are still being assessed on what you say and how you say it. Yes, be warm and friendly and not too stiff and stuffy; but never allow this to stray into informal and unprofessional. Don't say anything you wouldn't be happy saying on your application form!

Here are some other generic tips for interview technique:

Firstly, you must remember that interviewing is not a precise science and is, in many ways, unfair and stressful for candidates. I'm reminded of Churchill's assertion that "democracy is the worst form of government except all those other forms that have been tried from time to time": the interview process is the worst form of recruitment except all those other forms...

Secondly, you should try to anticipate the questions you're likely to get asked by each panel. If you can't, then I'll help you shortly. You should, therefore, be able to prepare answers to most of the questions you get asked. Rehearse them as much as possible before the day of the interview. For those questions you have not anticipated, rehearse how you'll react! How will you try to 'hide' or minimise any signs that you're thrown or stuck? Practice what you'll say to give yourself some thinking space and practice holding your body language in an open, relaxed pose.

Thirdly, try to appear at ease - though not too laid back - by thinking about how you're going to sit, what you'll do with your hands. If you get nervous and this manifests itself in shaking hands, then hold them steady on your lap. Try to stay as still as possible, avoiding incessant shuffling or repositioning. An open posture involves holding your hands out, palms forward, when making some statements. An interested posture involves sitting forward and making eye contact with the questioner. Use hand gestures and facial expressions to underline key points and to convey your enthusiasm and passion, but avoid performing a mime act which will distract the panel from your words. Above all, smile as often as possible!

It's worth monitoring the panel's reactions, too, but don't allow these to put you off. It's likely the panel will be making copious notes - this does not mean they are not listening attentively or interested in what you're saying. Don't be distracted or disappointed if you find yourself staring at a row of bald pates.

Fourthly, always try to relate your answer to the students. Talk about the importance of focusing on the students and on learning; try to avoid sounding too intellectual and speaking too theoretically. Avoid jargon and cliches like the plague!

Fifthly, do not speak for too long. Say succinctly what you think in answer to each question but do not provide a thesis on each topic. If the panel wants you to elaborate, they will ask you to do so. You could, if you're unsure, ask the panel if you've answered their question or if they'd like you to say more.

Sixthly, if you've forgotten the question or are unsure you're answering it directly, then stop and ask for the question to be repeated or explained.

Finally, do not feel under any pressure to ask questions of your own at the end, even if explicitly invited to do so. If you have a pertinent question, then feel free to ask it; otherwise, explain that all of the questions you had arrived with have already been answered. The panel is likely to be pleased with this: it is a long, tiring day for them, too!

Let's now take a look at some of the possible questions you could get asked by each of the main panels:

Finance
- What financial information would you report to the governing body?
- What measures would you take to minimise risk?
- If the school's budget was cut by £X next year, what would you do?

Curriculum
- What implications does the new National Curriculum

have for this school?
• What does 'personalised learning' mean to you?

Pastoral
• How would you engage parents and the community in school life?
• What would you do to improve our pastoral systems?
• How would you ensure that all the students at this school behaved?

Safeguarding
• What does safeguarding mean to you?
• How would you ensure that the school met its legal requirements for child protection?

In addition, you are advised to prepare generic answers on the following broad areas:

Leadership:
• What kind of leader are you?

Vision:
• What do you think are the key issues the school is facing and what will they be in three to five years?

Philosophical:
• What do you consider the advantages and barriers of the school's setting; what do you think about inclusion?; etc.

Ethical/political:
• When should the school exclude students?; what is our moral duty?; what is your attitude towards drug-taking/smoking?; etc.

Discipline/behaviour:
• How would you deal with a difficult situation such as

complaints against the headteacher?

Working relationships:
• What would you do if you disagreed with the headteacher's decision?

Experience:
• How has your previous role prepared you for this one?

Personal life:
• What are your hobbies?; how do you relax?; what do you think about work-life balance?; etc.

Now let's move on to the presentation...

The Presentation

Depending on the job you're being interviewed for and the school in which you're being interviewed, you might be asked to give a presentation to a group of staff.

Sometimes you will be given the presentation topic in advance and asked to prepare a ten or fifteen minute talk on that topic. However, it is not uncommon to be given the topic on the day of the interview so that you have to use some of your precious 'free' time to prepare the talk and so you are put under added pressure in order to test your resolve. In such cases, it is unlikely you'll be able to - or indeed will be expected to - use PowerPoint or any other resources.

If you are given the topic in advance, then you should prepare a few slides which will support your key points and you should ask (as far in advance as possible) if you'll be able to get access to a laptop and projector. Even when you have prepared presentation slides, however, and have been granted use of the ICT, you should expect it to fail you (sod's law) and should ensure you're not reliant on the technology.

A quick note on the use of PowerPoint: for a ten-minute talk, do not use more than about ten slides (ideally, far fewer than this); ensure each slide is professionally formatted (and devoid of SPaG errors) and that the text is kept to a bare minimum - you don't want the slides to detract attention from your wise words; you want the slides to summarise what you're saying or, better still, illustrate what you're saying with an image; avoid complicated animations which might not work on a newer/older version of the software and which will slow the presentation down.

Whether you're given time to prepare your presentation or not, you should try to keep it short and simple. You want to give a clear message; you do not want to deliver a verbal dissertation. The most memorable - and effective - speeches in history have been surprisingly short as we'll see in a moment.

In my book, *The Art of Public Speaking*, I talk at length about the language to use, the body language to adopt, and the structure to follow if you want to give a motivational, memorable speech. I want to share two extracts with you now. The first explores the best preparations to make (i.e. it is concerned with planning and writing a presentation). The second examines the best ways to deliver your presentation (i.e. it is concerned with your voice and body language).

There are three things to consider when writing your speech:

1. The big idea:

Your speech should set out one and only one idea. It has to be big enough to justify speaking about it but your speech must not get clouded or confused by other, less important, ideas or messages.

Your big idea can be exemplified by three points (three is the magic number). For example, your big idea might be "We have to change the way we work by..." And you might exemplify it by outlining 1. why the way you work now isn't effective, 2. how you want the way you work to change, and 3. what life will be like once you've made the change.

You should summarise your big idea at the end and, in so doing, you should make use of the dramatic pause. What do I mean? Well, any good joke is made up of the set-up, the pause and the punchline. The pause is what makes the joke work, without it the joke fails. It's just the same with your speech. You need to pause between your set-up and your punchline in order to highlight the punchline and heighten it in the audience's minds. For example, JFK did it when he said "Ask not what your country can do for you [pause] - ask what you can do for your country". You can do it by summarising your big idea thusly: "And if you take one idea away from my speech today it's this [pause] - " and summarise your big idea. Or maybe "What I need to say to you today is this [pause]" and make your declaration.

2. The structure:

How you organise your speech is important because your audience has to be able to follow your argument clearly and logically.

Perhaps the most important consideration when it comes to

structure is the overall length of your speech. And the simple answer is this: keep it short! A well-focused, succinct speech is the hallmark of a good public speaker. After all, no one ever complained that the speaker didn't go on for long enough! The only complaints you hear about the length of someone's speech is that it lacked brevity! If that wasn't proof enough, then remember this: Abraham Lincoln's Gettysburg Address was only two minutes' long; Martin Luther King's 'I Have a Dream' speech was just sixteen minutes' long.

The British pilot Lord Brabazon put it best when he said "if you cannot say what you want to say in twenty minutes, you should go away and write a book about it".

Another structural consideration to make is how to start your speech. The opening lines of a speech have to get the audience's attention, introduce you, the speaker, and provide some sort of overview of what you're going to talk about. Here are some useful 'do's' and 'don'ts' to bear in mind:

DON'T waste time on pleasantries and apologies: there is no need to tell your audience how delighted you are to be speaking to them today, nor is there the need to say you're sorry you haven't had much time to prepare or that you're feeling nervous. The pleasantries can go unsaid and the mistakes are best left hidden - be confident, assured, positive.

DON'T tell a joke: bringing humour into your speech is perfectly acceptable but humour should be natural and the result of your personality, or your self-effacing anecdote or the result of an interaction with the audience; humour should not be the product of a joke. Telling jokes is fraught with danger and is best left to professional comedians.

DO make lots of eye contact: Look directly at someone and engage them in eye contact before moving on to someone else and then a third person before speaking. This establishes you as a confident speaker, helps you to speak to individuals and not an amorphous crowd, and affords you time to calm your nerves. During the speech, continue to make eye contact, ensure you're addressing each point to someone in the audience. I like to draw an imaginary cross over the audience, connecting five people: one at each apex and one where the two lines of the cross meet in the middle. I then make eye contact with the five people in turn, moving from one to the other in a figure of eight motion. This ensures I make eye contact with every part of the audience and am not staring fixedly at the same point for too long.

DO make it personal: start your speech by telling a personal (real) anecdote to bring your idea to life. Show you care, take it personally and that you are human.

DO start with a bold statement or fact: say something provocative or pose a controversial question to get your audience thinking. You can qualify it later in your speech: the opening lines are no place to be shy!

DO make it relevant; do make it contemporary: perhaps start with an up-to-date reference, maybe refer to a story in the news. Then relate this to your speech.

Once you've started your speech, the main body of it should be divided into three sections: I always remember what the three sections are by using the mnemonic PEE where each letter stands for...

P = Point. This is an assertion, a statement or declaration

which summarises what you think and feel - perhaps it is a policy change;

E = Example. This might be a fact or statistic, or indeed a piece of anecdotal evidence, which supports and exemplifies your point - it provides the reason for a change of policy;

E = Explanation. This is an illustration of your point in practice and must be persuasive if it is to provoke the audience's feelings and thoughts. Explanations might take the form of stories, quotes, visual aids, a physical action or much more besides - but whatever form it takes, it should bring your point - your policy change - to life for the audience.

These three sections can be used in any order. For example, your speech might be structured as EXPLANATION, EXAMPLE, POINT. Here's an illustration...

• Start by telling a story which illustrates the big idea in your speech
• Then cite the findings of a survey which support the point you're making
• Finally, conclude with your big idea.

Here's an example I've invented about film piracy:

"On my way here this morning I was offered a copy of the latest James Bond film - which is still in the cinemas - on DVD for just £5. A recent study by the British Board of Film Directors has found that film piracy is on the increase and is costing the industry millions of pounds every year. It is time to change the law on piracy to bring tougher penalties on those buying - not just selling - pirated films."

The same sections could be shuffled so that the structure is" EXAMPLE, EXPLANATION, POINT:

"A recent study by the British Board of Film Directors has found that film piracy is on the increase and is costing the industry millions of pounds every year. On my way here this morning I was offered a copy of the latest James Bond film - which is still in the cinemas - on DVD for just £5. It is time to change the law on piracy to bring tougher penalties on those buying - not just selling - pirated films."

...and so on and so forth.

So, you've started well and have developed your big idea by employing PEE. What about the end? How do you ensure you leave on a high and make a big impression? Here are some more 'do's' and 'don'ts':

DON'T end with audience participation (unless you are explicitly told to do so). By all means, have a question-and-answer session during your speech if this is relevant. But don't end with one. Ensure you have time at the end to sum up your speech, to bring your argument full circle.

DON'T add further points at the last minute: use the last minute or so to sum up what you've already said and try to reinforce why it's important your audience acts on what you've said.

DO summarise what you want your audience to do - be explicit about the action they need to take next. Inspire them to act by calling upon the audience values and beliefs again, by reminding them what you and they have in common.

DO end with a bang: use a device such as a rhetorical

question, a quotation or a linguistic device which will stay with your audience once you've left the stage.

And finally on the subject of structure, you need to make sure your speech answers the following questions:

- What? In other words, what's your big idea, product or service? What goal do you want to achieve?
- How? How did you invent your big idea and how does it work in practice? How is it different to other people's ideas?
- Why? Why is your idea important and timely? Why is it needed? And why should other people get involved?

3. The language you use:

Strunk and White, in their book The Elements of Style, said that speeches "should contain no unnecessary words or sentences, for the same reason that a drawing should have no unnecessary lines and a machine no unnecessary parts. This doesn't mean that you must make all your sentences short or that you avoid all detail. But it does mean that you make every word count".

The language you use is also a prime consideration because spoken words are not the same as written ones. You should write your speech to be spoken not to be read. You probably write in a more complex way that you talk, use longer words and more complex sentence constructions. But to speak in such an elevated tone would sound unnatural and aloof. You should keep your language colloquial and easy to understand.

In the conclusion to The Art of Public Speaking I share eight basic tips - eight things to consider when delivering your presentation. Those eight tips are as follows:

1. Know your stuff!

Talk about what you know. Ensure you have a wealth of knowledge and experience on the topic of your speech. You should know much more than you say - behind your simple, effective communication should be detailed research and understanding.

2. Make 'em laugh!

Use humour, share personal anecdotes that entertain your audience so that they'll remember you and what you had to say. But shy away from telling jokes: this nearly always ends in disaster.

3. Practice makes perfect.

Rehearse your speech aloud several times (if possible) until you are confident you can cope without notes. Revise your speech as necessary as you identify ways it could be improved or made to sound more natural. Edit it down to avoid unnecessary tangents and the over-use of fillers such as 'hmm' and 'er' and 'sort of'.

4. Know your audience.

Research your audience beforehand (if possible) so you understand a little of them, their backgrounds, their prior knowledge on the topic of your speech, what makes them tick. If possible, greet some of the audience when they arrive because it's easier to speak to a group of people you know than to speak to a room full of strangers.

There's another reason why you should get to know your audience... you should be in control of as much of the event as possible, not just the words you're going to say. Beforehand, find out about the venue and about the audience so that you can try to tailor your speech to suit both. Familiarise yourself with the room and meet audience members before you speak, asking their names.

And then give the audience what they want...

The best way to impress an audience is to give them what they want. You can do this by showing them how your vision/mission/idea can help them to solve a problem they face or meet a target they strive for. For example, show them how your idea will get rid of something that burdens them, will save them time or money (or both), or how it will make their lives easier. Show them what they stand to gain as a result of your idea and how your idea is in line with their values and beliefs.

One effective way to do this is to use the Situation-Action-Result formula commonly employed by salespeople. Firstly, describe a person who faced a similar situation to that faced by the audience and show them how that person was adversely affected by their situation. Secondly, show how that person solved their problem by adopting your idea or proposal. Finally, show the positive outcomes the person achieved.

5. Know your environment.
Get to know the room you'll be speaking in, as well as the building and its surroundings. Practice using the equipment (where relevant) including the microphone. Test any technical equipment and visual aids you wish to use.

6. Try to relax.
Take your time, take deep breaths. Pause, smile. Try to convert your nervous energy into enthusiasm and passion.

7. Never explain, never apologise.
Don't apologise for your nervousness or a small technical hitch – the audience may not have noticed it. Instead,

concentrate on getting it right. And focus your attention away from your anxiety and concentrate on what you want to say.

8. It gets easier with time.

Get as much experience of public speaking as possible. Experience builds confidence, which is the key to effective speaking. It does get easier the more you do it and you will come to enjoy it and thrive on it. You'll get to the stage where you're not happy unless there's a microphone and a room full of people in front of you (which can lead to some pretty embarrassing moments)!

Don't be too hard on yourself if it doesn't go to plan...it is natural to feel nervous before and during a speech. Even the most accomplished of public speakers and actors get stage fright. And fear can be turned to your advantage: the adrenaline can become nervous energy which makes you appear passionate and enthusiastic. Enoch Powell used to advise avoiding the toilet prior to giving a speech because a full bladder makes you look lively and you speak with an urgency which is appealing and infectious: it makes your point seem more important and pressing.

If you want to calm your nerves, here are some ways to try temper your fear...

Firstly, the more prepared you are, the less nervous you will be. If you have practised your speech over and over so that you know it inside out, there is less chance of you forgetting any part of it and therefore less need to be nervous of mistakes.

Secondly, try to control your breathing - taking several slow, deep breaths helps counteract hyperventilation and calms your nerves.

Thirdly, remember that, no matter how nervous you feel on the inside, your exterior is unlikely to betray you. You almost always look calmer on the outside than you feel on the inside. So don't overreact, take a breath, take your time, hold yourself steady (hold the lectern if you need to) and let people think you're brimming with confidence. You might just convince yourself of that fact, too.

Now walk out onto that stage, stand tall at the microphone, look your audience in the eyes, pause, take a deep breath, and inspire...

So that's the planning and delivery taken care of. What about the content? As always, you need to prepare for the unexpected. Even if you are not given the topic in advance, you can do some preparatory work...

A useful starting point to your preparations is to ask yourself why you're being asked to give a presentation in the first place. The presentation exercise tends be used as part of the selection process for one of two reasons:

1. To assess your presentation skills: because school leaders need to be able to make impactful, coherent, accessible presentations to a wide range of audiences.

2. To assess your problem solving skills: because school leaders need to have the capacity to develop and 'sell' a solution.

Either way, you will need to balance the importance of what you say with how you say it. You will need to say something new, something insightful, something which demonstrates you're knowledgeable and a thinker, whilst also keeping your message short, simple, and impactful so as to leave a lasting impression on your audience.

If in doubt, make sure you seem confident, make sure you build rapport (use humour if possible - ideally of the self-deprecating kind -, and be magnanimous, recognising what your audience already does well or how privileged you feel to be visiting their school), and make sure you appear enthusiastic and excited by the prospect of working with them in the future. You want to be regarded as someone with whom the existing staff can work harmoniously and happily. You want to be regarded as someone who is considered, thoughtful, patient, and a good listener. You do not want to be regarded as someone who will arrive in September armed with hundreds of ideas about how the audience's precious school could be better.

You might be assessed for:

Your introduction: you'll be judged on how successful your greeting and self introduction is so think carefully about your opening actions and words. How will you approach the stage? Where will you stand? How will you stand? Where will you look when you start speaking and then throughout your talk? How will you say 'hello', explain who you are and what you're doing there?

Your connection to the audience: you'll be judged on how effectively you build rapport so think about how you'll endear yourself to the audience without being seen as weak or vacuous! You want to make the audience feel relaxed and perhaps even make them laugh, but you don't want to seem like a stand-up comedian who values style over substance and is devoid of intelligent ideas.

Your explanation of the task/purpose: you'll be judged on how well you structure your talk so that it is easy to follow and understand. It needs to be short and simple and you need each point you make to be recognised and understood. You do not want your audience to feel lost or confused. Think about using markers such as 'firstly', 'secondly', 'finally', and 'moreover', 'therefore', and 'on the other hand'. Make sure you summarise you key point(s) at the end and leave the audience thinking about what you have said.

Your delivery: you'll be judged on how confident you are; your use of pace, pause and emphasis; gaze, contact and gesture.

Your ideas: you'll be judged on what you say, how relevant what you say is, and how insightful it is about the school. You don't want to bore or patronise your audience by saying things about their school that they already know or which are obvious, but you do want to prove that you understand their school and recognise what it does well. You want to demonstrate that you have ideas but don't want to suggest you'll pursue your own agenda at the expense of everything the school has already achieved or does well. It's worth explaining that you have ideas but that you'd listen carefully to other people have to say before pursuing those ideas.

Let's turn our attentions to some of the topics you might be asked to present on...

Some panels favour a generic topic which allows candidates to make decisions about what is most relevant and important, and - by default - what is not. Generic topics also allow candidates to share their personal philosophies (and personalities) more easily. Other panels favour the unexpected/niche topic because it tests candidates' ingenuity and calls for more specific/tangible ideas that can catch the inexperienced candidate out.

Some possible topics to expect might be:
- How will you lead this department/school from 'good' to 'outstanding'?
- How will you add value?
- What do you consider to be the main challenges for the successful candidate and, if appointed, how will you address them?
- What is your vision for this department/school?
- Where will this department/school be in 3 years?
- What is excellence?

Accordingly, it's wise to prepare presentations on the following areas:
- What makes a constantly improving subject area/school?
- What structures enable positive change?
- What do you want for students and staff?

Such generic presentations can be adapted once you know the precise topic and once you've got to know the school better. During your preparations for interview and on the interview day itself, you might wish to tweak your presentation to include:
- The school's areas for development as identified in the latest Ofsted report and by the school's own self-evaluation
- Your own observations gleaned from your tour and from speaking to people

Now let's move on to the assembly...

The Assembly

You might be asked to give an assembly to a group of students. In which case, the first thing you'll need to consider is whether or not it constitutes a form of worship.

Next, think about the room you'll be giving the assembly in: is it small or large, does it have a projector and screen, will students be sitting on the floor, sitting on chairs, or standing?

Many of the considerations you'll need to make are the same as those you made when planning your presentation, such as: if you're using presentation slides then use as few as possible, ensuring each slide is well-formatted and kept simple but engaging with little or no animations; try to keep your speech short and simple, giving a clear message.

In short, my advice - if in doubt - is that an assembly should:
- Be kept short
- Be kept simple
- Give a positive message
- Hold students' attentions, perhaps via audience participation, and
- Build rapport, (you should smile and be friendly, perhaps humorous)

A good assembly articulates what it is that binds all the school's students and staff together. It is a means of rallying the troops, making them feel valued and respected, a part of a family. It can also be a call to arms, particularly ahead of important exams or sporting events.

I'm again reminded of Henry V's speech in Shakespeare's play. As I mentioned earlier, when Henry addresses his army before the Battle of Agincourt he says:

> *This story shall the good man teach his son*
> *And Crispin Crispian shall ne'er go by,*
> *From this day to the ending of the world,*

But we in it shall be remember'd;
We few, we happy few, we band of brothers;
For he today that shed his blood with me
Shall be my brother.

In other words, your assembly should articulate a "we are better together" message.

The Lesson Observation and Feedback

You may be asked to observe a lesson. This could be a real lesson or a video of a lesson. It's likely you'll also be asked to give feedback to the real teacher you observed in the flesh, or - in the case of the video - to a senior member of staff role-playing the part of the teacher.

The purpose of these exercises is to judge whether or not you're able to give clear, concise, and constructive feedback about the lesson's strengths and areas for improvement.

In terms of record-keeping, it's unlikely you'll be given a pro-forma to fill in and even more unlikely that you'll be asked to submit your observation notes - but always assume your notes will be read and analysed! Therefore, keep your notes short and simple. Above all, make them legible and professional: they should be observations of things you've seen (or not seen), as opposed to subjective comments.

When observing, it's good practice to:
• Sit whilst the teacher is talking or demonstrating
• Engage with the students whilst they are working
• Identify the different groups of students present in the room
• Look at what the students are doing and how they are reacting
• Look for evidence that all students are progressing in

relation to the learning outcomes and their ability, and identify whether some groups are progressing less well than others

• Consider how the teaching is impacting on the learning of pupils through the planning and delivery of the lesson

At the end, summarise your main points (in perhaps a handful of bullet-points) including the main strengths and the main areas for improvement.

When giving feedback - whether it be to a real teacher or someone in character - remember to be polite, professional, and friendly throughout. Even if the lesson was dreadful, there is nothing to be gained by being confrontational or rude! Think carefully about the language you use: you do not want your choice of words to be in direct conflict with your judgment of the lesson. A useful word to use is 'interesting'. 'Interesting' doesn't imply good or bad - a lesson can be interesting because it is wonderful or because it is as traumatic as a car crash. I usually begin feedback sessions by saying, 'Thanks for allowing me to spend some time in your classroom today, it was a really interesting lesson'.

You should always remember that the lesson you have observed is unlikely to be typical of the way that teacher teaches day in day out - not least because he/she was being observed. An observed lesson can be very stressful and often teachers will offer a 'showcase' lesson aimed to impress but which bears little relation to their everyday practice. And often the 'showcase' lesson is not as good as an everyday one because it's been over-planned, over-thought, and therefore becomes over-wrought.

It's also wise to remember that the observed lesson was a

mere snapshot - it was not representative of the teacher's entire professionalism or abilities. Your feedback should make this point explicit - just as you would differentiate between a student and his/her behaviour when chastising them for misbehaving; you should differentiate between the teacher as a person and professional, and the snapshot of one lesson you've observed.

In the best feedback sessions, the observed teacher talks a lot more than the observer. Not only is this good practice because it encourages the teacher to reflect on their own performance, it also helps the observer avoid a difficult situation in which they have to impart bad news and invite argument!

Some useful questions with which to start the session are as follows:
• What went well? What aspects of the lesson are you most pleased with?
• If you were to teach that lesson again, what would you do differently and why?
• Can you describe the level of learning that took place in the lesson?
• Did all students make progress (or 'did all students learn something', or 'did all students close the gaps in their learning?') and how do you know?

Once you've facilitated a discussion around these questions, ask the teacher to summarise the strengths and areas for development as they see them.

Once the feedback has been completed, you should move the meeting towards action. Whatever the feedback, there is always follow-up action to be taken. If the lesson is excellent then the action might be to enlist the teacher to share their good practice, to help colleagues to improve the quality of their teaching. Perhaps the teacher could lead a professional development session or video part of a lesson and share it with colleagues in a staff meeting. If the lesson is less than good then the action might be to engage the teacher in some professional development, perhaps observing a colleague and trying new approaches in their own classroom.

Whichever path is taken, it is important to end the feedback session with a clear plan of action, complete with reasonable timescales, and an agreed method for the teacher to report to you the progress they are making against this action plan.

Once the actions have been summarised, it is time to thank the teacher for allowing you to observe his/her lesson and for being professional throughout the discussion.

Occasionally, you will be asked to give lesson feedback to the selection panel rather than the teacher. In which case, you can focus on:
•   Outlining, clearly and succinctly, the main strengths and weaknesses of the lesson
•   Explaining how you'd share the good practice you've seen in this lesson with other teachers and how you would use your observation to move the quality of teaching throughout the school further forwards.

The Student Panel

Many schools include a student panel in the selection process. Often, the panel consists of the school council, each member of which has prepared - sometimes with guidance - a question for you. Every school is different but when I have used a student panel, I have never asked students the question 'Who would you appoint?'; indeed, I have always been clear that they are not part of the decision-making process. Instead, I explain that students are involved because it's important that the candidates spend some time talking to students in order that the candidates can learn more about the school. In reality, I use the student panel for one reason: to see how well candidates respond to young people - which is, of course, of vital importance for school leaders.

With this in mind, my advice is this: don't get preoccupied by the questions and your answers, focus on showcasing your ability to build rapport with students.

Here's a few suggestions about how you can do this:
• Turn the questions around: ask students what they want
• Use students' names as often as possible, make lots of eye contact and smile
• Speak plainly and sincerely, avoid jargon - but don't patronise students
• Chat with students more informally at the end, ask them some questions of your own, take an interest in them and their school
• Compliment them on their school, articulate your eagerness to join their school family.

Simulations (e.g. A Meeting)

As the name suggests, simulations (and by that I mean assessment tasks which simulate situations you're likely to find yourself in if appointed, such as team meetings) are entirely artificial. A team meeting, for example, is usually - though not always - a pleasant affair in which colleagues work together, collaborate and share. A simulated meeting, however, pits rival candidates against each other in an Apprentice-style battle to prove who's the cleverest, most decisive and determined future leader.

Or is it? I think the best policy to adopt in these situations is to acknowledge the artifice, accept that it's not real and that your rivals are likely to scrap it out to be top dog by volunteering to chair the meeting before you've even had time to take your seat, then by enthusiastically commenting on everything everyone else says whilst allowing everyone else very little time to say anything at all before barking, "Yes, good point Steve, really good point... now, let's remember that our objective here is to..."

Let someone else be chair, let someone else be time-keeper. They're probably not going to be very good at it and can do far more harm than good by raising their heads above the parapet.

I sense you disagree with me. After all, you cry, I'm applying for a school leadership role so surely I should show the panel that I am a leader, that I can take charge of meetings? Yes and no. What is leadership? Haven't we already established that good leaders are calm, kind and considerate, that good leaders are also good listeners? Well, now's the time to demonstrate your kindness and your listening skills.

I'm not advocating taking a back seat and refusing to engage with the task. Please don't sit back and fold your arms, say nothing and snigger at the candidate who volunteered to be chair because he just repeats what everyone else says only with the words in a slightly different order. But let the others fight it out at the beginning whilst you climb up to the moral high ground, find a comfortable knoll on which to sit, then demonstrate that you are capable of keeping your head when all around you are losing theirs: stay calm and collected throughout, be positive and open (both orally and in your body language); stay focused on the task in hand, don't be lead down blind alleys or along tangents; respond naturally, trying to rise above the artifice and act as you would normally act; and don't get distracted.

The purpose of a simulated meeting or group discussion is to assess your team working skills not necessarily the quality of your contributions. I'm not suggesting you can put forward ridiculous, fanciful ideas but I am saying that it's how you conduct yourself not what you say that matters most. So focus on your body language - open and friendly, relaxed and confident - and on being polite and professional, kind and considerate towards your rivals.

In practice, this might mean the following:
• Bring the best out in others
• Build on what others say
• Keep the discussion moving in the right direction
• Assimilate the information effectively
• Summarise and conclude the actions the group has agreed
• Stay focused on the objectives of the task and keep to the timings
• Stay calm and polite.

Written Exercises

You may be presented with a written task such as writing a report or analysing data. Whatever the task, my strongest advice is this:
• Keep your written language short, simple, and precise
• Focus on a small number of key points, do not attempt detailed, intricate analysis
• Ensure your observations or comments lead to action, state what you would do and why
• Prioritise the actions you propose to take according to

the impact they will have on student learning

Let's take a look at a handful of the written exercises you're likely to get...

The in-tray exercise

You might be given a set of simulated emails, letters, memos and telephone calls. You'll be asked to prioritise these pieces of correspondence then explain how you'd respond to them. Such a task requires you to justify your decisions according to the impact they will have on student learning; demonstrate how you'd delegate effectively; and show how you'd monitor and review your actions as well as the actions of others.

The in-tray exercise tests your ability to respond to priorities. You'll be presented with a scenario which seeks to simulate the real tasks of the post for which you're applying. The scenario often takes place at the start of a term or week and often includes the unexpected absence of key personnel.

The in-tray typically includes between ten and fifteen items. The items are a mixture of urgent and important items, urgent but unimportant items, as well as routine issues and some irrelevant or incidental items. You'll be asked to complete the in-tray by placing the items in rank order of urgency and importance, explaining the reasons for your ranking and how you would deal with each item. You'll be given a finite amount of time to complete this task in order to reflect the hustle and bustle of school life. The exercise is designed to provide real insights into your sense of leadership and management.

The follow-up

Sometimes, a follow-up activity will draw out a handful of items from the in-tray and you'll be asked to expand upon your initial answers. You'll be invited to set out all of the options that you consider are available to you.

The purpose of this activity is to test the breadth of your understanding, as well as your ability to be innovative.

The briefing note

A third task may ask you to take one item from the in-tray and write a briefing note or letter to one of the school's stakeholders, perhaps the headteacher or the chair of governors.

This tests your communication skills. This task places a premium on your capacity to manage upwards, your ability to see the school from someone else's perspective and your capacity to understand what key information is needed by the recipient of the note.

Data analysis

If you're asked to carry out a data analysis exercise, don't worry if the data is new to you or if you're not a numbers person! Try to sort the wheat from the chaff, cut through the complexity of the data and identify key trends and issues. At its simplest, you're likely to be looking for the biggest and/or smallest numbers, and for any anomalous numbers in a sequence.

Keep your analysis simple and straightforward and use the key trends in order to create a relevant action plan, showing what you'd do to address the trends you have identified.

Try not to appear too rash, too quick to rush to judgment. Acknowledge that all data is flawed and you would need to triangulate information from several data sources before being confident of a decision.

And that's the last hoop through which you'll have to jump. You can glance at the schedule and feel a sense of relief that you're nearly there.

But don't get complacent just yet...

All of these circus tricks were mere warm-up acts for the big finale... so, drum-roll please, it's time to welcome to the stage, the one, the only, the final interview!

M J Bromley

Chapter Three:
The Final Interview

Let's get the hard work over and done with first...

The biggest question you're likely to get asked is this: What would you do to improve our school?

The School Improvement Question

A good starting point - without knowing the school's specific context - is to consider what, generically, makes a school outstanding. What are the common ingredients shared by all the most successful schools? Understanding the key features of an excellent school is helpful in trying to determine what the school you're applying to work in already does well and what it needs to do better. It's also useful because it can provide you with a framework around which to build your action plan. I have a top ten list we can begin with...I think the most successful schools each share the following ten characteristics:

1 Effective leadership: an outstanding school needs

effective leadership, leadership which is strong and has a clear direction, leadership which is inclusive of all staff and students.

2 *A shared vision:* an outstanding school needs a shared vision, a clear idea of where it is headed (a common goal) and how it is going to get there; an outstanding school also needs an effective school improvement plan and effective systems of monitoring and evaluating performance which are understood by all staff.

3 *Data is understood, used effectively and leads to action:* an outstanding school is one in which data is understood by all staff and in which data is used to drive improvements, to aid progress and to avoid underachievement. Spurious data is ignored and data is used to help inform decisions though it is not used in isolation, it is triangulated with other evidence to paint a complete picture.

4 *All students make progress:* an outstanding school is one in which students make good or better progress, where students are given aspirational targets and where intervention is early and effective and personalised, where student progress is tracked and students are rewarded for hard work.

5 *A rich curriculum which includes a raft of extra-curricular activities:* an outstanding school is one in which there is a broad, engaging curriculum which meets the needs of all students and provides a gateway to future success. An outstanding school is one in which there is a variety of engaging and appropriate extra-curricular activities which extend the boundaries of learning and provide a safe environment for young people. An outstanding school also provides extra-curricular activities which actively encourage community involvement and participation, and widen students' knowledge and experience.

6 Staff are supported and motivated: an outstanding school is one in which staff are well-supported and cared for, and where they are motivated to work hard and take pride in a job well done. An outstanding school is one in which professional development is taken seriously and staff are valued and have the tools they need to do their jobs.

7 Purposeful environment: an outstanding school is one in which there is a well-organised and attractive environment – an environment which is physically engaging and conducive to learning; as well as metaphysically engaging with effective (i.e. not bureaucratic and not time-consuming) systems and structures.

8 Vulnerable students are identified and supported: an outstanding school is one in which vulnerable children are identified, their needs are known and in which staff are appropriately trained and have the skills to support them effectively.

9 Students are challenged and encouraged: an outstanding school is one in which students are challenged and encouraged to work hard and are rewarded for their efforts, where students are engaged in their learning but where there are also clear, effective sanctions in place. An outstanding school is also one in which students of all abilities and interests (not just the most able and the least able) are known, catered for, and supported to achieve their full potential.

10 Parents and the community are informed and contribute: an outstanding school is one in which parents have a voice and can contribute to school life, and where the community and the school work together for the benefit of all. An outstanding school is one in which governors take an active interest in school life, are knowledgeable about what happens in school, and strike the right balance between support and challenge: they are a critical friend working as servants of the school - indeed, acting as ambassadors of the school in the wider community - but are not afraid to question its direction.

In addition to this list (which I've compiled and tweaked over many years and which is intended to be 'future proof', focusing as it does on the most fundamental characteristics of successful schools rather than fads and fashions), I've also been inspired by how Judith Little (an education researcher at the University of Berkeley in California) defines a successful school. Based on the research she conducted in the 1980s, she says that all the successful schools she's seen, do the following four things (the broad sentiment is hers; the words and interpretation are my own):

1. Teachers talk about teaching
In other words, meetings are used - not for business and administrative tasks - but for talking about pedagogy. Teachers swap ideas, discuss lessons and students, and share good practices.

2. Teachers observe each other
All teachers engage in a programme of peer observations and give constructive feedback to each other. Often, teachers also team-teach.

3. Teachers plan together
As an advocate of 'less is more' when it comes to lesson planning (Ofsted no longer expects, or indeed accepts,

lesson plans and - in my humble opinion - lessons are nearly always better when they are fluid and flexible rather than over-planned) I interpret this to mean the following: teachers share their ideas for medium-term planning (what we need to teach and in what order), make their resources available to each other and scrutinise each other's assessment records and students' books, giving each other constructive feedback.

4. Teachers teach each other

Staff meetings are transformed into Professional Learning Communities where teachers share practices with each other. Teachers try out new ways of teaching, video their lessons and play the video to other teachers, sharing what worked and what didn't. Together, teachers help to raise the quality of teaching and to ensure greater levels of consistency across the school.

In order to ensure that the above ingredients are expertly blended into a mouth-watering banquet, school leaders need to create effective structures in which:

- There is a clear vision of what is trying to be achieved
- Targets are realistic and achievable
- True delegation is offered and senior staff are empowered to make decisions
- Effective communication systems are in place;
- Purposeful meetings are called; meetings are minuted and actions set
- Paper work is kept to a minimum
- All staff know exactly who does what
- Actions are delivered within the context of the school improvement plan
- Students are at the centre of any decisions and changes
- There are effective monitoring and evaluative procedures in place at all levels
- There is clear value for money in terms of the school's

effectiveness and efficiency.

Your research into the school will have provided you with some notion of how far along the journey to outstanding the school is and to what extent the school has begun building the above structures and how embedded those structures currently are (I say 'embedded' rather than 'finished' because the school improvement journey has no terminal destination... the last thing a school should do when it is judged 'outstanding' by its Ofsted overlords is relax, sit back and bask in the warm glow of approbation! The journey continues and arguably along the toughest terrain yet because being sustainably outstanding is no mean feat!)

Allow your research to inform you which of the above structures you discuss and to inform you of the way in which you discuss them. For example, if you feel the school has already adopted a clear vision then say what you'd do to ensure that vision continues to be relevant and of value, and what you'd do to help realise that vision. If monitoring and evaluation has improved in recent years then say what you'd do to build on the good work of the school, what you'd do to help and support the school to make further improvements.

As with every answer, it's a judgment call: you need to be pragmatic and make a decision about what the school is looking for. Is it looking for someone who'll complement the current SLT and who'll embody the school's existing values and vision; or is it looking for someone with an outsider's perspective and a keen critical eye who'll add challenge and encourage the school to - oh no, I'm going to say it - 'think outside the box'.

Unless you're applying for the headship of a school which is in dire need of change, a need which is clearly recognised by the governing body and local authority (this will be made clear in the chair of governors' letter) then steer clear of the all-out attack-mode, i.e. the Bob the Builder approach (exclaiming that the school is broken and you can fix it). But navigate a path somewhere between all-out attack and limp platitudes. Go for the 'it's good but could be even better if...' approach. Talk about what you hope to learn from the school if you're appointed as much as what you can teach the school. In short: be magnanimous.

Once you've articulated what you'd do to improve the school, you may be asked how you'd approach the change. A quick word about change management is therefore useful...

The Change Management Question

Eric Hoffer once said that "In an age of great change, the learners inherit the earth while the learned are beautifully equipped to deal with a world that no longer exists". In other words, change is not only an inevitable, natural part of life, it's essential if we are to keep on getting better.

In order to demonstrate that you can help move the department or school forwards, you will need to show the panel that you have a good grasp of change management.

Although to differing extents, all leaders are leaders of change. But, whereas most leaders enjoy the challenge of change (after all, it's why we want to lead: to make things better), many other people do not share our enthusiasm. Any effective process of change management should, therefore, begin with recognising why some people do not like it. Here is my suggested list as food for thought...

People are resistant to change because:
- They are anxious of the impact it will have on their jobs
- They feel they have tried it before and it didn't work
- They fear it will mean more work for them
- They do not understand the need for change, they like the status quo
- They fear failure
- They are scared by the pace of change and by being out of their comfort zone
- They fear change will prove too costly or a waste of time and money

All of these points are valid. Sometimes people like to moan or resist change because they're lazy or difficult; but most of the time they resist it because they have very sound and logical reasons to do so.

The best way to overcome these barriers is to:
- Be open and honest about the need for change
- Explain the rationale behind change, and
- Outline the benefits of change for everyone.

And this requires the following skills:

- Patience and self-control
- Balance
- Communication
- Problem-solving
- Personal ownership

Above all, effective change is characterised by effective consultation.

I'm sure we've all been part of a consultation process which is anything but consultative! Consulting, after all, is not necessarily the same as acting on other people's ideas. You can consult then do whatever it was you intended to do in the first place. But effective consultation is genuine consultation. Any leader who believes he or she has all the answers is likely to be disappointed! If a problem shared is a problem halved, then an idea shared is an idea refined and improved countless times. You should start the process of change by outlining your ideas and by inviting feedback and suggestions. You should respond to each and take it seriously. You should be open-minded about what might work and what might not.

Finally, the following conditions enable effective change to happen:

Effective leadership – leadership which is democratic, which acts as a role model, which supports and encourages others. Why? Because effective leadership leads to people feeling involved and valued, provides broader, richer insights and ideas, and helps improve staff morale, as well as recruitment and retention; effective leadership also shares responsibility, leads to less stress, higher standards of teaching, effective collaboration and more honest relationships in which problems are aired and resolved faster.

Inclusive culture – a culture in which people know they can contribute and overcome barriers together, in which everyone is encouraged to play a part in driving the school's change agenda.

Broad collaboration – collaboration between schools, stakeholders and other organisations which helps embed a culture of openness to positive change.

Change teams – working parties which are inclusive and representative of all areas of school, a team which acts as a communication channel between the senior team and the workforce and which makes staff feel involved in their school.

In *How to Lead: The second edition of Leadership for Learning* I share a change management cycle which has five stages as follows:

1 Mobilise
2 Discover
3 Deepen
4 Develop
5 Deliver

This cycle is a means of helping you plan for change. For example, the mobilise stage is about airing your initial ideas, and establishing a working party of interested people who will help you to develop your ideas further and trial new ways of working before those changes are rolled out to all staff.

There are plenty of other change management cycles and processes out there which are worth considering but nothing trumps the human approach I advocate above of being open and honest and consulting genuinely and widely at all times.

The Leader or Manager Question

At this stage it's worth taking a step back to consider the job title: you're applying for a school leadership position not a school management position. This might sound like semantics but it's not. Leadership and management are words often glued together like 'salt and pepper' and 'knife and fork' but they are actually quite different. Yes, it is true that most leaders are appointed because they have a proven track record as good managers; and, yes, it is true that good leaders need to continue practising their management skills. But nevertheless the two are different. Whereas managers bring order and organisation; leaders bring change and challenges. Managers are concerned with the short-term; leaders with the long-term. Managers solve problems and achieve goals; leaders pose questions and generate options and opportunities.

In *How to Lead: The second edition of Leadership for Learning*, I express this idea more pithily when I say that:
* Managers are operational, and
* Leaders are strategic.

Managers need a range of skills including: communication, organisation, operational leadership, managing difficult staff and managing difficult situations.

Leaders need strategic vision (to be able to see clearly where they and their school are going, to be able to aim high and share their passion and determination with others, to be able to communicate their plans with enthusiasm and clarity) and strategic planning (knowing where their school is now, where they want to go and how they're going to get there).

If you're applying for a leadership position, be careful to articulate what you understand by the term 'leader' and if you're asked to define your leadership qualities, be sure to mention the importance of strategic planning!

Generic Questions

Every school will take a different approach and it is impossible to predict which questions you will be asked. However, it is wise to prepare answers to the following generic questions (the wording of which may differ, but semantically they will remain the same):

What are your values?

What are your strengths

What are your areas for development?

What are your biggest achievements to date?

What are your proudest moments?

What impact have you made to date?

What are your ambitions for this job?

What skills are needed of effective leaders?

What's your unique selling point?

When answering each of these questions, be honest! Don't be smug or cliched and - for example - claim that your biggest weakness is the fact you work too hard. Stick to tangible things such as your knowledge of whole-school finance or governance arrangements. Equally, don't be too smug about your strengths. Show humility, perhaps some humour too.

As I say above, for each of the weaknesses you share (and don't share too many: perhaps two at most), you should - whether invited to or not - explain what you're already doing to address it. For example, if finance is a weakness, explain that you're working with your school's finance manager to improve your knowledge and understanding of income and expenditure, and reporting procedures.

When outlining what you have achieved, remember to state what impact those achievements have had on students. In other words, support your answers with evidence. As mentioned above, your evidence could come from:

- Data
- Ofsted reports
- Awards, success marks and prizes
- Reports from a local authority advisor / SIP
- Work used as exemplar materials by the LA / other schools
- Personal appraisals / performance management
- Feedback from parents, students, colleagues, governors and others

Above all, remember to be personal, genuine, and to show you are human!

A quick note on body language. I know that your mind will be busy thinking about what to say and how to say it but try to pay some attention to the way in which you sit. Try to strike an open posture - avoid defensive body language such as folding your arms or sitting back. Sit forward with your arms open or on your lap.

Remember to stay hydrated throughout the interview. Pour yourself some water before you begin (if this hasn't already been done for you) and utilise the time you're accorded whilst being asked questions to take a drink and lubricate your mouth! If you need to pause mid-answer to take a sip, do so!

Equally, if you need to pause mid-answer to think about what you're saying, to clarify in your own head what you want to say, then do so... if you need more than a few seconds, then explain to the panel that you need to take a moment to consider the question fully so that you're able to give the panel a clear, succinct answer. Try: "I'd like to take a moment to think through my answer to that question if you don't mind because there's so much I could say, I'd like to articulate an answer of appropriate clarity and brevity" (or something that means the same thing but is slightly less pompous).

If the question was long, confusing or unclear, don't be afraid to ask for it to be repeated or rephrased. Try: "That was a detailed question which deserves a detailed answer. I wonder if you'd be able to rephrase it or to clarify what you're looking for in reply so that I can do it justice".

Taking time to clarify what is being asked and to think through how you're going to respond is wise because less is more: you should try to keep your answers short and focused. If the panel wants further clarification or wishes for you to elaborate, they will ask.

Competency-Based Questions

Some interviews are competency-based and you will be asked to recount some successes you have achieved in the past as evidence that you possess the experiences, knowledge and skills required in the job for which you're being interviewed. Competency-based questions - in other words, questions which seek to identify your behaviours and skills - have been common in the private sector for many years but are now becoming more popular in education, too.

If asked to talk about a project you have lead, or a change you have successfully made in your current role, you will need to be specific and talk through, step-by-step, what you did and why. But you will also need to relate those experiences to transferrable skills and qualities, skills which you'll be able to use in your new job.

Your examples should focus on your leadership style and how your leadership has made a difference. Your examples should also demonstrate that you are self-critical and reflective: you should say what you learned from the experience and what you'd do differently next time.

Although you're unlikely to be told in advance what competencies you'll be asked to discuss, as always there are ways to prepare for the unexpected. Firstly, you should consider the skills listed on the person specification. Secondly, you should consider the skills that all good leaders almost always possess. Broadly speaking - in no particular order and by no means exhaustive -, I'd advise having ready examples of actions you've taken which provide evidence of:

- Working with colleagues
- Improving teaching and learning
- Raising attainment
- Improving pastoral care and student wellbeing
- Strengthening links with the community
- Working with parents
- Taking responsibility for improving your own skills and expertise
- Creating links with other schools or colleges
- Dealing with a child protection/safeguarding issue
- Improving resources and/or departmental planning
- Overcoming difficulties/disagreements with a colleague

Some of these categories overlap and it's feasible - perhaps wise if you're to keep a clear head - to use one example as evidence of more than one category. For example, an example of how you've improved teaching and learning might also be an example of how you've improved planning, taken responsibility for your own development, and how you've raised attainment. If you use the same example for several categories, then be careful to relate the skills and attributes to the competency you're being asked to demonstrate.

In a competency-based interview, it's advisable - for each of your examples - to practice your answers to the following questions:

As you know, one important thing we are looking for is.........We would like you to think back to an actual context where this competency/quality was involved. What was the situation?

What led up to it?

Who else was involved?

What were you trying to accomplish?

What was the first thing you did?

Tell us a little more about how you went about that. What were you thinking at that point?

Tell me more about the sequence of your thoughts. What was your part in all of this?

Tell me about a particular aspect of that situation which stands out in your mind.

Had you thought about that beforehand?

Tell me what you said.

What was the response to that?

What were you feeling at that point?

What was the next thing that you did?

Can you explain that a little more?

How did it turn out?

Is there anything else you would like to add about what you did/did not do in that situation?

What did you learn from that?

Is there anything which, in retrospect, you would now do differently?

Any interviewer who asks all of these questions and interrupts you as frequently as this list suggests should not be interviewing, they should be working for the secret services interrogating terrorists! I provide these cues merely as possibilities, as useful thinking points or spurs which may help you to formulate a more detailed answer and which may encourage you to be more self-reflective about what you did, why you did it that way, and what worked and didn't work.

In addition to thinking of an example for each of the categories of competency-based questions I proffer above, it might be wise to prepare answers to the following generic competency-based questions:
• How do you lead?

- How do you 'sell' your ideas?
- How do you delegate?

For each example, be clear about:
- The rationale - why you did what you did
- The actions you took
- The impact of your actions (with evidence).

I find the SOARA technique helpful when sharing examples of past successes. SOARA stands for:

S = situation (what was the problem, what needed changing, how did you know?)
O = objective (what did you set out to achieve?)
A = actions (what did you actually do, in chronological order?)
R = result (what was the outcome, how did you know?)
A = aftermath (what did you learn, what was successful, what would you do differently, how can you apply this learning to your new job?)

Or you could use the simplified STAR system where STAR stands for:

S = situation (the problem)
T = task (the resolution)
A = action (what you actually did, what obstacles you faced and how you overcame them)
R = result (the outcomes and what you learned)

Some competency-based questions are pegged to the National Standards (which I discuss in more detail above). Let's take a moment to consider some of the questions you might be asked...

The Six Realms of School Leadership Questions

It's possible you will be asked questions about the general qualities and values expected of school leaders, as well as their roles and responsibilities. To help you prepare, here is a list of possible questions against each of the six realms of school leadership I set out earlier in this book:

Setting a vision for the future
1 What, based on your experience to date, do you think equips you for this role?
2 How would you describe your leadership philosophy and style and how do you think you could use it effectively to support the development of our teaching staff?
3 How will you establish yourself in your first term in post?
4 How will you support and contribute to continuing to develop the vision and direction for the school?
5 Which aspects of the role will be your strength and which will be more challenging?
6 Describe your role in a situation where significant change was needed to be implemented to bring about improvement?

Being the lead teacher
1 We have consistently poor attendance / behaviour from a small number of pupils. How would you address this issue?
2 This school has an issue with attendance. Can you talk us through your ideas in relation to improving attendance?
3 How would you propose to monitor the quality of teaching in this school?
4 What are your ideas about and experience in improving the quality of teaching?
5 What strategies do you think are the most effective in monitoring the effectiveness of staff?
6 What does effective leadership and management of teaching and learning look like for you? Answer the

question making reference to your previous experience

7 Based on your knowledge of the school, what are the key areas for development?

Working with developing others

1 We have a large staff at the school – how are you going to make sure that all staff are working towards the same goal?

2 What is the most effective CPD that you have participated in? What made it effective?

3 What constitutes good performance management?

4 What in your view is the role of performance management? Describe a successful performance management meeting for yourself or one you have led

5 What are the principles that underpin building a learning community? Give an example in your current context, of how you have put these principles into practice?

6 How are you going to manage if you have a serious disagreement with a more senior colleague on a point of principle?

Leading the organisation

1 What do you think are the main organisational challenges for this school and how do you think they might be tackled?

2 How do you want to work with the governing body?

3 How will you ensure that the priorities reflected in the school improvement plan are the priorities of all key stakeholders?

4 Given current initiatives and areas for development, if you were given £15000 how would you advise that it should be spent?

5 Talk to us about a project you have managed, within your current context, to plan for and implement change.

6 Describe the processes and practices you have used to develop whole school policy?

7 From your experience what do you see as the heart of effective financial management?

Managing the team

1 Based on your experience to date, what have you learnt about effective evaluation and how will you encourage the staff to evaluate the work of the school objectively?

2 In your role as a senior leader, how will you ensure that all members of staff are clear about accountability; and what will you do if they don't?

3 In your experience, what are the most effective ways of ensuring that self evaluation is an integral part of the work of the school?

4 How will you hold staff accountable for children's learning outcomes?

5 What do you think your contribution can be to working in partnership with the governing body to ensure that they can hold the school to account in an informed and appropriate way?

6 How have you ensured that the members of the teams you have led are clear about their role, responsibilities and accountabilities?

Developing external links

1 Based on your experience, what are the most effective ways of increasing parent involvement with the school?

2 How will you encourage parents to improve pupil attendance and punctuality?

3 Based on your experience, what are the most effective ways of involving parents and the community in supporting the learning of children and in defining and realising the school vision?

4 Talk to us about your current experience of working in collaboration with other schools, agencies and community groups. What is the impact of that work on pupils learning?

5 What are the benefits and challenges of effective multi-agency working?

6 Talk to us, from your current experience, about how you

have created and promoted positive strategies for challenging racial and other prejudice and dealing with racial harassment.

It's not the Spanish Inquisition...

The final interview will probably consist of fewer questions than you might imagine, say six. But each of the six questions is likely to be open and enabling, and your response to each is expected to be around five minutes long. The questions may become progressively more challenging and demanding.

You might be asked to give a ten minute presentation before the interview begins (either as your only presentation - see above - or as an additional presentation to the formal one you gave on day one of the process) and your first question may respond to something you've said in your presentation.

The first 'scripted' question might be along the lines of, 'Having learned more about our school today, what experiences have you had and what have you learned from them that will prepare you for this role?' Note this question is in two parts: you need to ensure you answer both elements, detailing not just your relevant experience but also what you learned from it. After all, experience without insight is of little value. Good candidates will outline their experiences, explain what they learned from them and then relate that learning to the school and the role for which they are being interviewed.

Another common question tackles the skill of change management. For example, you might be asked the following: 'Take one example of major change you have delivered in your current role. Describe the key elements of this change and say what worked well and what didn't work so well.' This may be followed by a supplementary question such as, 'Reflecting on this experience, what have you learned about managing change, as well as about yourself, that would add value to the role you're applying for?'

Again this is a two part question which requires a two part answer. Firstly, you should have a good example of change management (see 'The Change Management Question' above) and should articulate your general approach to change. Then you should highlight what worked well and explain the reasons for this success, whilst recognising that change is often uncertain and does not always proceed smoothly. Secondly, you should acknowledge the areas of difficulty and analyse how things went awry. Then you should set out what you learned from this experience in terms of attempting future change and in terms of your capacity to plan and develop change, as well as your capacity to engage with others. Strong candidates may wish to add a third dimension by applying their learning to the new role.

M J Bromley

Chapter Four:
Conclusions

And that's it. You're ready. All that remains for me to say is thank you for reading and 'good luck'. School leadership is many things. It is a privilege, a pleasure, one of the most important jobs you could ever hope to be blessed with. The one thing school leadership is not, is dull! Each new day is different to the last. Each new day is a learning experience, something to be warmly embraced. Above all, school leadership enables you to make a real difference.

Once you're appointed, take a moment to reflect, to remind yourself why you applied for the job in the first place. Re-read your vision statement. Memorise it, say it out loud to yourself like a mantra. Keep your vision centre-stage, let it be your guiding star, a means of celestial navigation, ever-present in the - sometimes stormy - skies above you. Allow that vision to motivate you to get up in the mornings, and to keep you going when it seems that everyone and everything has set a course against you.

Remember that you're in the position of being able to truly

change lives, to genuinely and profoundly shape the futures of all the young people in your care. There can be no more important job than this. So enjoy it, cherish it, keep it safe. And the best way to do this? You've guessed it... Be human. Be true. Be you.

Good luck!

ABOUT THE AUTHOR

M. J. Bromley is an education author and journalist with over eighteen years' experience in teaching and leadership. He works as a consultant, writer, lecturer, and consultant, speaker, and trainer, and is a school governor.

Find out more at www.bromleyeducation.co.uk

Follow him on Twitter: @mj_bromley

M J Bromley